KEYWORD
ACCELERATOR
PLAYBOOK

KEYWORD
ACCELERATOR
PLAYBOOK

*A TACTICAL SEO KEYWORD RESEARCH
& CONTENT PLANNING GUIDE FOR
BOOSTING YOUR WEBSITE'S RANKINGS,
TRAFFIC & EARNINGS*

STEPHEN HOCKMAN

KEYWORD ACCELERATOR PLAYBOOK
A TACTICAL SEO KEYWORD RESEARCH
& CONTENT PLANNING GUIDE FOR BOOSTING YOUR
WEBSITE'S RANKINGS, TRAFFIC & EARNINGS

ISBN 979-8-83513-091-7

FIRST EDITION

Contents

For all the bloggers, niche website builders & affiliate marketers who are driven to make this SEO thing work.

Your freeway to success starts here.

INTRODUCTION

Welcome to the SEO fast lane for getting higher website rankings, traffic, and profit!

I'm Stephen Hockman, creator of the *Keyword Accelerator Playbook* and a full-time blogger at SEO Chatter.

My journey with SEO and Internet marketing started in 2005. And back then, I was just like any new website owner:

Completely lost about what to publish and stuck in the slow lane with every aspect of my site.

My initial strategy was to pluck ideas out of thin air and write articles I thought people in my niche would be interested to read. I figured, if it was something I was curious about, then others would be (hopefully) searching for that same kind of content on Google and land on my website to get it.

Well, that idea flopped.

Most of the articles I wrote barely got any visitors at all. And the ones that did get some Google search traffic had no noticeable pattern whatsoever.

I was literally shooting in the dark with every piece of content I produced.

But then I stumbled across something that gave me a glimmer of hope to keep pushing forward.

It was called Google Adwords. And Adwords was a relatively new product by Google that allowed advertisers to create text-based ads that would appear in the search engine results pages (SERPs) for specific keywords. Essentially, these paid ads would show up at the top of the SERPs before the organic search results, which, at the time, were called the famous "10 blue links".

What was great about Adwords back then was that it let you see the precise monthly search volume for any keyword in Google's database. (Today, it's just a broad range.) Plus it was free to use. That meant you could easily find out which topics users were trying to find information about online and the exact number of searches being performed without paying any money to get those insights.

This was an amazing breakthrough for me because I was on a super tight budget, yet could finally start publishing content with somewhat of a keyword strategy. Instead of writing about anything under the sun in my niche, I finally knew what topics I should actually be targeting to get people to my website from Google's search engine.

But that surge of hope quickly faded.

A lot of the articles I published still didn't rank high in SERPs. And that was extremely frustrating as a new blogger/niche site builder/affiliate marketer, which is an accurate summary of the complete mash-up of everything I was trying to be at that time. Some days I was so paralyzed by the horrible state of things that I would avoid writing anything new for weeks on end. But eventually, I would think about that burning desire I had for creating my first website:

To make endless streams of passive income.

It was that flash of inspiration that would kick me into high gear and drive me to publish a large batch of new content that may or may not have ended up ranking in the top 10 blue links on Google. However, even with the Adwords keyword research tool at my disposal, I was still lost on the freeway without knowing where I was going.

It wasn't until I failed miserably over and over again for several years that things finally clicked. Those failures led me to figure out what my biggest mistakes were.

What I slowly realized was that I was approaching the whole content publishing game in the wrong way. And there was a basic set of rules that the most prolific online publishers were following that made everything a whole lot easier for them to obtain faster success.

What I didn't know back then was that I was swimming in a red ocean. And where I needed to be was in a blue ocean.

Chan Kim and Renée Mauborgne, authors of the book *Blue Ocean Strategy: How to Create Uncontested Market Space and Make the Competition Irrelevant*, coined the terms "red oceans" and "blue oceans" to denote the market universe. Basically, red oceans are where companies try to outperform their competition to grab a greater share of the existing market. But in a blue ocean, there's no competition at all or very little competition in the market, making it much easier to succeed as a business.

That same blue ocean concept applies to SEO and ranking websites in search engines like Google, Yahoo, and Bing. A blue ocean is where there's very little competition in the SERPs for a target keyword and you can often rank your content high without a lot of effort. However, a red ocean has a lot of direct competition in the SERPs and it can become a feeding frenzy among SEOs and website publishers trying to one-up each other to gain the top-ranking positions. And in many cases, it can almost impossible to break through to the top 10 spots.

Unbeknownst to me, most of the articles I was publishing were targeting red ocean topics.

When I found a good keyword in Google Adwords with a high search volume, I got super excited and wrote an article on it. But what I wasn't aware of at that time was that many of those high search volume keywords were impossible to rank for in the SERPs.

The competition for those terms was just too fierce among the other SEO sharks. It was a bloody red ocean where my content had no chance of survival. And trying to compete was both a waste of precious time and resources.

It wasn't until I found a unique tool called Market Samurai that I understood what was going wrong with my keyword research strategy. Market Samurai was one of the first keyword research tools on the market that provided daily search volume and recent trend data for the keywords in any niche, taking the data directly from Google. This tool also gave you an SEO competition score for each search term and a list of important SEO metrics for the top 10 ranking URLs in the SERPs.

Getting access to Market Samurai was a game-changer for my entire keyword research process. It was the springboard for getting me out of the shark-infested red ocean and into the empty blue ocean where I could finally thrive with my website.

Sadly, Market Samurai doesn't exist anymore but if you had a chance to use it, then you'd understand how most keyword research tools you find today are based on a similar framework.

(Note: I ended up switching to a few other keyword research tools that are much better for analysis which you'll find out about in the "Recommended Keyword Research Tools" section.)

At this point in my SEO journey, I was having much better success with my website. I was doing a great job uncovering easy-to-rank keywords and getting a lot more of my articles into the top 10 positions on Google. Learning how to do proper on-page SEO was also a huge contributor to this success.

But I still had three significant problems.

The first issue was that I was taking a shotgun approach to how I selected keywords to target on my website. I literally had no clue which terms to pick. (Perhaps you can relate to this?)

My only criteria at the time was that the keyword had to have low competition in SERPs. Other than that, the keywords I chose could have been about any random topic in my niche. And that strategy eventually stopped working as topical relevance became more important to Google's ranking algorithm. This caused my web pages to slide down in the SERPs.

The second issue I suffered was that some web pages earned me a lot of passive income through affiliate marketing (and eventually display ads once that revenue model became available) while others were barely making a few pennies.

Sometimes I would pour my heart and soul into a new article with high hopes of it delivering stacks of cash to my bank account. But more often than not, those articles would just rake in a couple of dollars each month and a majority of my income was coming from only a few URLs where I accidentally struck gold by picking some highly-profitable keywords.

The final issue that almost put me out of business altogether was that I had no content publishing strategy in place. I basically opened up a keyword research tool, found a good keyword to target, then wrote an article on that topic.

Sometimes I spent an entire day looking for a single keyword and a week or more actually getting the content written and published. My publishing schedule was all over the place with absolutely no consistency whatsoever. (Does that sound familiar?)

One week I might have published 2 articles, 0 the next, and 3 a month later. Everything was so haphazard with my writing schedule. And that inefficient way of publishing content was gravely holding back my website's growth.

Now, fast forward to today.

After clunking my way through many different websites, I eventually came up with a powerful keyword research process that solved all of my problems from before. This definitely didn't happen overnight though, as I had been doing SEO since 2005 and had plenty of years of trial and error to figure it all out.

But now my process is dead simple for finding the very best keywords to target for my websites that keep them swimming a big beautiful blue ocean with organic search traffic rising month-over-month while also squeezing every ounce of profit out of each visitor who lands on the sites. There's no second-guessing why my content doesn't rank well in the SERPs because most of it hits the top 10 positions with ease.

I also ended up developing a reliable content publishing strategy that transformed my shaky passive income side hustle into a rock-solid steady business that keeps me in the fast lane. Now every website I create follows a proven publishing plan for success where I know exactly what I'm going to write, when it will be published, and how much content I need to reach my traffic and income goals.

This trouble-free method removes all the guesswork out of how to take the very best keywords I've found using a simple keyword research tool and put them into a content publishing schedule that's guaranteed to deliver results.

Having a plan like this in place has made writing so much more enjoyable and profitable for my business.

So why am I telling you all of this?

Because those strategies are exactly what you're going to discover in this *Keyword Accelerator Playbook.*

I'm literally giving you my exact blueprint for how I do keyword research day in and day out in the fastest and most optimal way. And it works with practically any keyword research tool on the market.

In fact, I encourage you to spend as little money as possible on one of these tools, which is the exact opposite of what a lot of other SEOs out there are saying to do. Instead, they insist you have to pay for expensive software like Ahrefs to have any chance at keyword success. But I'm here to tell you that's simply not true.

I've built and sold websites for more than $100,000 using nothing more than cheap keyword research tools you'll find out about later in this playbook. So don't let anyone fool you on this.

I'm also teaching you how to set up a content publishing schedule so you have a complete plan to follow to reach your website goals faster. This is an area where I haven't found any other SEO expert, blogger, niche site builder, or affiliate marketer sharing information.

Oddly, the entire Internet marketing industry is practically devoid of teaching website publishers how to create a content publishing schedule to run their online business more successfully. And that's one top reasons why I had to include this crucial information inside this playbook.

After you go through the step-by-step instructions on how to create a content publishing schedule with ease, you'll be set up for a lifetime of achievement for publishing content in the most effective way on any website you create.

My ultimate goal is to help you get your website into the SEO fast lane so you can enjoy higher website rankings, traffic, and profit.

It was a great feeling to get these processes that took me years to refine out of my brain and put down into words for you to read and benefit from. That's because I know in my heart how much these strategies can help transform your life as a website publisher if you put them into practice and stick with them for the long term.

Not only will you be able to experience faster growth in website traffic, but you'll also know what it takes to achieve higher earnings through display ad revenue and affiliate commissions.

Plus, you'll have the foundations in place for creating an effective content publishing schedule that can keep you on track to grow your website beyond your wildest dreams.

I hope that gets you excited.

Because it excites me to share it all with you in this *Keyword Accelerator Playbook*!

So let's hit the road and see how far you can go.

Your SEO mentor,
Stephen Hockman
Founder of SEO Chatter

SECTION 1
KEYWORD RESEARCH

What Is Keyword Research?

Keyword research is the process of finding and analyzing terms your target audience is typing into search engines like Google, Yahoo, and Bing with the purpose of using that data to create content those people want to read and to help guide the search engine optimization (SEO) process for it.

The basic keyword research process consists of a few steps:

- Enter a term into a keyword research tool.
- Sort through the list of suggested keywords to find ones you like.
- Compare the keyword metrics to make sure a term is worth your time and effort to pursue.

Why Is Keyword Research Important?

Keyword research is important because it can reveal vital information to grow the traffic and revenue for your website.

The keyword research process can help you discover which words and phrases your target audience is actively looking for in the search engines, the competitiveness of those terms, the amount of traffic each one can potentially bring to your website, and an estimate of how valuable those keywords can be for your business.

Keyword research is a crucial part of the content creation process because it helps you develop a more effective content publishing strategy. Although it can be fun—*or even cathartic*—to write about topics you're interested in sharing with the world, the fact is there's a high probability that you'll end up with a bunch of articles on your website that people are not interested in reading if that content is not centered around specific keywords.

In other words, all of the effort you put into writing and publishing content that you *think* is worthy of being found on search engines like Google, Yahoo, and Bing will most likely be wasted because your articles won't get the traffic or attention they deserve.

Understanding how to do keyword research is also beneficial for your website's SEO.

A good keyword research strategy can help you make better research-based decisions for optimizing new and existing content to improve its rankings in the search engines for specific terms. Without doing keyword research, you would have no idea which words or phrases to include in your content to gain favor with the ranking algorithms. Instead, you would just be guessing at what search engines like Google want with no clear direction on which keywords actually matter the most for your website's SEO.

Additionally, keyword research can help you determine which terms are worth pursuing or not for your website based on the level of competition in the search engine results pages (SERPs).

For example, some keywords are very difficult to rank high for in the SERPs unless the website has a strong Domain Authority and/or individual Page Authority scores. And to secure those top spots in Google, Yahoo, and Bing often requires a strong backlink profile that many newer websites cannot compete with. This is a prime example of swimming in a red ocean that's full of bloodthirsty sharks.

However, the opposite is also true.

Some keywords can easily be ranked in the top 10 SERP positions without needing powerful SEO metrics for the domain or individual web pages. But you wouldn't know this unless you did good keyword research. This process is the only way you can find hidden gems like that to gain more website traffic without facing fierce competition in the SERPs. And this is a perfect example of swimming in a blue ocean with very few sharks around, which is exactly where you want to be as a website publisher.

Another important thing to think about with keyword research is the value that each phrase can bring to your business. The fact is every keyword is worth a price for both website publishers and advertisers. Some terms are worth a lot more money to both publishers and advertisers because those keywords offer a higher return on investment (ROI).

For example, a keyword that has high commercial intent, like "buy car insurance", could be worth $50 or $60 for each Cost-Per-Click (CPC) a car insurance advertiser is willing to pay to get a hot lead to their website. On the other hand, some keywords have little to no commercial value at all (e.g., $0.10 or less CPC value) and are only good for bringing in new website visitors for brand awareness.

Fortunately, the keyword research process can help you uncover the best terms that can deliver the highest ROI for each article you publish and optimize for SEO.

With all that being said, when you understand how to do keyword research in the most efficient way, as it's outlined later in this playbook, you'll be able to develop a more effective content publishing strategy that can get you closer to your website goals.

The fact is that well-thought-out keyword research can drive tremendous results for your online business.

Not only does it help you increase your website's overall visibility in the SERPs, but it also works to bring in higher levels of traffic and total revenue through data-driven insights.

In other words, you'll no longer have to guess what works to achieve better—*and faster*—results for your website when you're publishing quality content based on keyword research and optimizing it for SEO.

Types of Keywords

Now that you understand what keyword research is and why it's important, the next thing you need to know is the various types of keywords you can target with your content. This will help you gain better control over the keyword research process and make it easier to create a content publishing strategy that works best for your website.

There are three primary types of keywords that cover the entire range of search queries that are performed on search engines like Google, Yahoo, and Bing. And each of these keyword types is based on a concept called user search intent.

User search intent refers to the purpose of an online search (i.e., the objective the searcher is trying to accomplish).

For example, a person looking to buy a new pair of shoes has a different search intent than someone who wants to know how to clean their dirty shoes. The first person would want ecommerce options for making a purchase online while the second person would need instructional information that teaches how to perform a task.

That's why it's important to understand the different types of keywords and their user search intents so you know which categories of content you should be targeting on your website.

Knowing the exact type of keywords you want to focus on during the keyword research process will help streamline the work. It will also stop you from aimlessly picking keywords to write articles about with no real plan in place for long-term content publishing success.

The following sections will explain everything you need to know about the three primary types of keywords based on user search intent.

Informational Keywords

Informational keywords are used to meet the search intent of people who are looking for an answer to a specific question or to get general information about a topic.

These types of SEO keywords typically start with "who", "what", "when", "where", "why", "how", "are", "can", "do", and "does".

An informational keyword doesn't have commercial search intent, so these types of terms are not often the best choice for making direct sales through a web page. Informational keywords are at the top of the sales funnel where people are beginning to research a particular topic by gathering more details. However, these types of keywords in SEO are still valuable for brand awareness and lead generation because you can answer questions about your industry, individual niche, products, or services, and provide informational content that educates your target market on topics that can bring them deeper into your sales funnel.

Examples of informational keywords include:

- What is off-page SEO?
- How do keywords work?
- Does pizza have high calories?

Example informational keywords continued…

- When is the next presidential election?
- Why are whales so big?

Transactional Keywords

Transactional keywords are used to meet the search intent of a person who is ready to purchase something. These terms have the strongest commercial value and are commonly known as buyer keywords.

Types of SEO keywords in this category typically include modifiers like "best", "top", "cheap", "review", "buy", "purchase", and "for sale".

The person searching for transactional keywords is often at the bottom of the sales funnel which makes these keywords a good choice for direct sales on a website because the user search intent is so strong for purchasing a product or service.

Examples of transactional keywords include:

- Best SEO company
- Top keyword research tool
- Baby jogger city mini reviews
- Buy stocks online
- Rookie baseball cards for sale

Navigational Keywords

Navigational keywords are used to meet the search intent of people who know what they want but are not exactly sure how to find it online.

Common examples include when a searcher is looking for a particular website, brand, product, or service. The person knows it exists but needs Google, Yahoo, or Bing to help them find the root domain, contact information, specific product or service page, etc.

Navigational keywords fit in every part of the sales funnel (top, middle, and bottom). When a user types a navigational keyword into a search engine, it means that person is likely familiar with the company and wants to find something specific from that business. Therefore, the user search intent could be either informational or transactional.

That's why it's important for every brand to have optimized content for navigational keywords that include their company's name, individual products, and services.

Examples of navigational keywords include:

- YouTube
- Petco customer service

Examples of navigational keywords continued...

- SEO Chatter website
- JBL extreme 3
- Dave's auto body repair

Keyword Length

In addition to keyword types, SEO keywords also come in several lengths that are classified by the number of words in the search term.

Understanding these classifications can help you develop a better SEO strategy for your content and get the most effective use out of a keyword research tool.

There are three primary lengths for keywords that cover the entire range of search queries that are performed on search engines like Google, Yahoo, and Bing.

The following sections will explain everything you need to know about these keywords lengths.

Short-Tail Keywords

Short-tail keywords are 1-2 words long, have the highest search volume, and have the most competition in the SERPs. They're also not very targeted terms because the user search intent is often ambiguous. That makes it hard to write and optimize the perfect type of content to satisfy the user's needs for these keyword lengths. Plus, red oceans are full of short-tail keywords.

Therefore, I typically don't recommend you target short-tail keywords for your website content unless you can find a hidden gem with massive traffic potential or earnings in addition to super-low competition.

Examples of short-tail keywords include:

- Dogs
- Cat food
- Internet marketing
- Search engine optimization

Typically, search engines like Google, Yahoo, and Bing serve a mixture of content to users in the SERPs for short-tail keywords because the algorithm doesn't know exactly what people are looking for with these terms.

For example, a user searching for the word "dogs" may be trying to find the definition for the word, see pictures of these animals, get a list of popular dog breeds, or find local places to adopt a dog as a pet. As you can see, short-tail keywords are very ambiguous which is why they can be hard to target with a particular article.

It's often not worth the time, money, or effort for a small to mid-size website publisher to compete in the SERPs for short-tail keywords. You can achieve a lot more—*and faster*—success by writing and optimizing content for medium and long-tail keywords.

Medium-Tail Keywords

Medium-tail keywords are 3-4 words long, have a moderate search volume, and average competition in the SERPs. Terms with this length are more targeted than short-tail keywords because the user search intent is easier to establish. This makes it possible to write and optimize articles for medium-tail keywords that can bring in a good amount of website traffic and earnings.

As you're doing keyword research, you'll find a mix of both red oceans and blue oceans that are full of medium-tail keywords.

Examples of medium-tail keywords include:

- Dogs that shed
- Cat food recipes
- Internet marketing strategies
- Search engine optimization for beginners

Long-Tail Keywords

Long-tail keywords are 5 words or longer, have the lowest search volume, and least competition in the SERPs. They're also the most highly targeted keywords for SEO because the user search intent is so specific. This makes it extremely easy to write and optimize content for long-tail keywords that fully satisfies the needs of the search.

As you're doing your keyword research, you'll find that long-tail keywords are almost always swimming in deep blue oceans. Because these terms are so long, it's rare to see much competition for long-tail keywords, which makes them excellent choices for gaining easy website traffic.

Examples of long-tail keywords include:

- Dogs that are good with kids
- Cat food that is safe for allergies
- Internet marketing advantages and disadvantages
- On-page search engine optimization strategy

The Most Important Keyword Metrics

Now that you have a good understanding of the various keyword types and lengths that make up every kind of search query imaginable in the search engines, it's time to move on to a list of criteria that can help you quickly assess the value of the terms you find during the keyword research process.

When it comes time to choose the right target keywords to write articles about for your website, there are several important keyword metrics you need to consider to create an effective content publishing strategy. Diving into a keyword research tool to brainstorm new ideas is great, but you won't have as much success if you're not analyzing the right keyword data.

If you think back on the story I told in the introduction about using Google Adwords to find keywords to target, even though it was free, I was still shooting in the dark because it didn't provide all of the necessary data to make the right decision on if I should focus on a specific keyword or not.

There are three objective metrics you can use to make better data-driven decisions for selecting the best keywords to target for your website. The following section will explain everything you need to know about those data points.

Search Volume

The first important keyword metric is search volume which refers to the average number of searches a particular keyword receives in a given time frame. Some keyword research tools allow you to check the search volume for a set of keywords based on a set period of time, like the previous 3 months, 6 months, or 12 months, to get a better idea of how the search volume is trending.

Keyword search volume is also averaged over a set time frame to provide you with a general clue of the overall volume.

For example, a keyword may have received a total of 1,000 searches over the previous 3 months but the tool will report an average search volume of 330, which is roughly:

1,000 (searches) ÷ 3 (months) = 330 (average search volume)

In reality, the keyword may have been searched 700 times in month 1 of the selected time frame, 200 times in month 2, and 130 times in month 3. But on average, the keyword gets 330 searches per month over a 3-month time frame.

So keep that in mind because monthly search volume

can fluctuate based on seasonality and trends throughout the year. Also, keyword search volume is just an estimate. It's never 100% accurate.

Just because a keyword research tool reports an average of 5,000 searches per month for a particular keyword doesn't mean your website will actually receive that number of visitors. Nor does it mean that 5,000 searches are performed each month for that term as you previously learned.

However, the average search volume for a keyword is still your best metric for evaluating the overall user interest and potential traffic to your website.

Now, there are cases where a keyword research tool reports a 0 search volume for a target keyword but it actually ends up delivering 100s or even 1,000s of visitors to a website. Again, that's because the search volume data is never 100% accurate and sometimes a keyword may be too fresh in the index to report accurate volume.

Additionally, a keyword might surge in popularity before the keyword research tool updates its database. However, if you're trying to create an effective SEO content publishing strategy for your website that can guarantee the best long-term results, then you should not focus on 0 search volume keywords.

You may hear other website owners talk about how much success they've had by targeting keywords like that, but the truth is the ROI on those terms is vastly unknown and you could end up writing articles that barely bring in any website traffic.

Therefore, it's better to choose keywords that have a proven search volume (e.g., 100 or more searches per month is a good place to start) even if your site may get more or less than that number of visitors per month.

Keyword Difficulty Score

The second most important keyword metric is the keyword difficulty (KD) score which estimates how hard it might be to rank for a specific keyword on the first page of Google's search results.

The KD score is calculated based on many factors; however, the backlink profile strength of the ranking URLs in the top 10 positions is typically given the most weight. Keyword difficulty scores range from 0-100. The higher the KD score, the harder it typically is to rank on the first page of Google for a search term because the competition is much more difficult based on the quality and number of incoming backlinks to the top-ranking URLs.

The KD score is a powerful SEO metric you can use to evaluate potential keyword terms for your website because it helps you avoid search terms that require a lot of backlinks to rank in the top 10 positions.

Therefore, the KD score should play a significant role in your keyword selection process if your goal is to rank your website in search engines like Google, Yahoo, and Bing for more relevant keywords with the least amount of effort.

For example, it's not uncommon for a web page to rank in the top 10 positions on Google for a target keyword with a low KD score within a few hours or even a day after the page has been published. That's because keywords with a low KD score do not require a strong backlink profile to get ranked on the first page of the search results. Typically, all you need is good on-page SEO with your target keyword in the right locations on the page and well-written content that satisfies the user's search intent.

By combining those factors together (low KD score, on-page SEO, and content focused on user search intent), you can often grab the top positions in the SERPs even with a website that has a low Domain Authority and/or individual Page Authority scores.

Cost-Per-Click Value

The third, and final, important keyword metric is cost-per-click (CPC) value which is an advertising revenue model where advertisers pay publishers each time a user clicks on a text-based or display ad.

The CPC value refers to the actual price advertisers pay for each click in a pay-per-click (PPC) marketing campaign. This is vastly different than the cost-per-mile (CPM) model where advertisers pay a fixed price for every 1,000 impressions an ad receives regardless if a user clicks on the ad or not.

CPM is also known as revenue-per-mile (RPM) or earnings-per-thousand-visitors (EPMV).

Essentially, advertisers that use digital marketing platforms like Google Adwords to gain more customers and increase sales will bid a certain amount of money for their online ads to show up in Google's search results pages as text ads and through Google's Discover Network as display ads on publishers' websites.

The main purpose of CPC ads is for a brand to get its products and services in front of potential customers without having to do the work of ranking organically with SEO in the search engines. In other words, advertisers can pay money on a cost-per-click basis to be featured above the organic search results in Google and on publishers' websites without worrying about using SEO to get traffic.

The reason why you should focus on the CPC value during the keyword research process will be explained later in this playbook in the section called "Keyword Accelerator Formula (Overview)". But for now, just know that advertisers are willing to pay more money to get brand exposure for certain keywords versus other terms in search engines like Google, Yahoo, and Bing. And knowing this can work to your advantage because you can use that data to pick more profitable keywords for your website.

Recommended Keyword Research Tools

As you learned in the last section, there are three important keyword metrics you need to consider when selecting the best search terms to target on your website. And the only way to get that full range of data is to use a good keyword research tool.

Now, if you were to do a search on Google right now for the phrase "keyword research tool", you would find more than 100 different options that promise to help you find great keywords to target for your website. But there are a lot of inefficient tools out there that don't give you everything you need to make the right data-backed decision for your website.

The two most common metrics missing from a lot of keyword research tools on the market include the keyword difficulty (KD) score and cost-per-click (CPC) value. Some tools may have one or the other but not both. And you don't want to waste money on a tool that doesn't have all three important keyword metrics: search volume, KD score, and CPC value.

Keep in mind that some keyword research tools do have their own proprietary version of the KD score and label it by another term, such as SEO score, difficulty rating, etc. Also, the pricing for keyword research tools is all over the place with many of them being quite expensive. Some software even has extra features that are completely unnecessary for the average blogger or website publisher but serve as a way to justify the higher cost.

Fortunately, you don't need to spend a ton of money on a keyword research tool or waste a lot of time trying to figure out which software is going to be the best to help you find perfect keywords for your website.

After being in the SEO industry for 15+ years, and testing numerous types of software, I've discovered there are three powerful—*and inexpensive*—keyword research tools you can use to find great terms to target on your website. In fact, these are the same tools I use on a daily basis to find the best keywords for my own articles. So you know they've been fully tested and guaranteed to include the most important keyword metrics you need for success.

Next, you'll find out what those keyword research tools are as well as the top benefits each one has to offer so you can decide for yourself which one you want to use moving forward.

KWFinder

KWFinder is my favorite keyword research tool that's offered by Mangools. I use it for every keyword research task because it allows me to find the best terms my target audience is searching for on Google and quickly analyze the most important keyword metrics to help build out a monthly content publishing schedule.

KWFinder also comes bundled with a full suite of other SEO analysis tools at a very affordable price. It can take care of most, if not all, of your SEO exploration needs as a website publisher.

And in my opinion, you don't need any other extra tools as a blogger, niche website builder, or affiliate marketer if you invest in the Mangools SEO suite.

Mangools includes:

- LinkMiner (for backlink analysis)
- SERPWatcher (for keyword rank tracking)
- SERPChecker (for analyzing the SERPs)
- SiteProfiler (for analyzing important SEO metrics and getting content insights)
- KWFinder (for keyword research)

Top Benefits of KWFinder:

• Search volume data can be switched between the last 3, 6, or 12 months.

• Keyword difficulty (KD) score uses a color code for each difficulty level to make it easy to find low-competition keywords fast: Green for easy, Yellow for possible, Orange for hard, and Red for very hard.

• Each keyword displays a SERP overview with the top 10 ranking URLs along with key SEO metrics like Domain Authority, Page Authority, Citation Flow, Trust Flow, Number of Backlinks, Link Profile Strength, and Estimated Visits Per Month.

• Offers 3 ways to research keywords: Related Keywords, Google Autocomplete, and Questions.

• Includes a search volume trends graph for each keyword so you can view user interest throughout the year.

I encourage you to try KWFinder for FREE to experience firsthand everything it has to offer you through my affiliate link: **seochatter.com/kwfinder**

LowFruits

LowFruits is another favorite keyword research tool of mine that helps you find keywords where you have the easiest chance to rank in the top 10 positions on Google. It literally removes all the guesswork and time-consuming tasks of digging through hundreds of keywords to find quick wins for SEO rankings and traffic.

This tool fetches the top-ranking URLs and shows you how many weak websites are in the top positions. Typically, these sites contain User Generated Content (UGC), like Quora or Reddit, which is easy to outrank by writing a good piece of content that's well optimized for SEO and meets user search intent. LowFruits also reveals ranking websites with a low Domain Authority score which is a powerful sign that you can also win those top-ranking positions without needing many backlinks.

If you want to invest in a single keyword research tool that doesn't come with any extra SEO software like Mangools provides, then LowFruits is your best—*and cheapest*—option. LowFruits offers a pay-as-you-go pricing model, so you only pay for the keyword data you need without being locked into a monthly or yearly contract. Even though I pay for a monthly Mangools subscription, I still use LowFruits to find super-easy keywords to target.

Top Benefits of LowFruits:

- The Weak Spots feature instantly shows you how many weak websites are ranking in the top 10 positions on Google. Plus, it uses color codes for the types of websites in the SERPs: Green for a Domain Authority < 20 and Blue for a Forum or UGC content site.

- You can perform your initial keyword research with a seed keyword to get a list of all of the related keywords with their search volume metrics without using any credits. Then you can select which keywords you want to analyze for Weak Spots and CPC data so you don't waste any of your credits.

- You can filter keyword reports with features such as Weak Spots in the top 10 or top 3 positions, Sites with DA < 10, UGC sites in the top 3 positions, Search Intent, Search Volume, CPC Value, and more.

- Includes the average word count for the top-ranking URLs so you can quickly assess how much content you need to write for a particular keyword.

You can try LowFruits for FREE and GET 10 FREE credits using my affiliate link: **seochatter.com/lowfruits**.

Keysearch

Keysearch is another great keyword research tool that has a few additional SEO tools built into it like KWFinder but has its own unique spin on things.

With Keysearch, you can get keyword suggestions, analyze keyword difficulty, do competition analysis, track your website's rankings, and more.

What makes it truly stand out from other tools on the market is the Content Assistant tool that suggests topics and related keywords you can include in your articles to help them rank higher on Google. That feature alone is why so many people choose to use this product.

Top Benefits of Keysearch:

- Keyword difficulty (KD) score for each search term has color codes for each difficulty level. Colors range from various shades of blue to red to indicate the SERP competition which ranges from very easy to very hard.
- Offers 9 ways to research keywords: Related Keywords, Keysearch's Own Database, Google Suggest, Bing Suggest, Youtube Suggest, Amazon, Etsy, Ebay, and Pinterest.

Top Benefits of Keysearch Continued...

- Each keyword displays a SERP overview with the top 10 ranking URLs along with key SEO metrics like Domain Authority, Page Authority, Number of Linking Domains, Number of Backlinks, and Number of Dofollow Links.

- Includes a Competitor Gap tool to compare different competitors and find common keywords that their websites are ranking for but your site is not.

- Includes a Rank Tracker tool to track up to 150 daily keyword rankings.

Try Keysearch for FREE and get a 20% discount by using coupon code KSDISC through my affiliate link: **seochatter.com/keysearch**

Keyword Accelerator Formula (Overview)

Once you have access to a good keyword research tool that reports the three most important metrics (search volume, keyword difficulty (KD) score, and CPC value) you can then use that tool to guide your keyword research strategy in a way that achieves the best—*and fastest*— results for your website.

I call this process the "Keyword Accelerator Formula" because it's a fail-safe method for uncovering easy-to-rank keywords that can give you a speed boost in obtaining more profitable website traffic.

What's great about this strategy is that it strips out all of the extra noise that many keyword research tools have that can distract you from your ultimate goal:

To choose keywords as fast as possible to accelerate website traffic and profit for your business.

Gary Halbert, a pioneer in direct response marketing, once said, "Money is attracted to speed." And this concept applies specifically to the keyword research process.

The faster you can find good—*and profitable*— keywords to target, the more traffic—*and money*— you can earn as a website publisher.

Below, I'll go over the basic steps for the *Keyword Accelerator Formula*. Then in the next section of this playbook, you'll get the complete how-to guide with in-depth step-by-step instructions for how to put this strategy into practice from start to finish.

The Keyword Accelerator Formula

Low KD + High SV + High CPC = Optimal KW

Low KD: Find Keywords with a Low Difficulty Score

The first element of the *Keyword Accelerator Formula* can help you unlock a ton of easy-to-rank keywords that can drive more traffic to your website without worrying so much about the competition. By starting here, you'll only be analyzing keywords that can put your website in a blue ocean.

Essentially, you want to start the keyword research process by finding relevant keywords for your website that have the lowest keyword difficulty (KD) score. That's because this metric indicates that those search terms have the lowest competition in the SERPs.

As mentioned previously in this playbook, you can often rank high in the search engines for low KD score keywords just by doing good on-page SEO and writing content that meets user search intent. Content that's optimized for keywords with a low KD score typically does not need a large number of backlinks to rank in Google, Yahoo, and Bing. And some articles will not need any backlinks at all to rank in the top positions in the SERPs.

High SV: Narrow Your List by the Highest Search Volumes

The next part of the *Keyword Accelerator Formula* is to sort through the list of keywords with the lowest KD scores to find the terms with the highest search volumes because these keywords offer better opportunities to get higher levels of traffic to your website with the least amount of effort.

For example, a keyword with KD score of 20 and search volume of 10 is not as attractive as a keyword with a KD score of 20 and search volume of 1,500. The keyword with 1,500 monthly searches has the potential to send you a lot more website traffic for the same amount of effort it would take to write and optimize an article for the keyword with only 10 searches per month. Therefore, you should always pick the keyword with the higher ROI.

By first narrowing your list of low KD keywords to only including the highest search volumes, you can discover a treasure trove of potential keywords that are easy to rank in Google, Yahoo, and Bing that can drive more traffic to your website without it needing to have the highest SEO metrics to compete in the SERPs. Keywords that contain low KD scores + high search volumes can put your website in a deep blue ocean with very few, if any, competing SEO sharks swimming in the water.

High CPC: Compare the Cost-Per-Click Value for Each Keyword

The final element of the *Keyword Accelerator Formula* can take your website to a whole other level if you're monetizing with display ads or affiliate products. By comparing the cost-per-click (CPC) value for each keyword in your list, you can make better choices as to which terms are best to target for financial gain.

As mentioned earlier in this guide, CPC is an advertising revenue model where advertisers pay publishers each time a user clicks on a text-based ad or display ad. The CPC value refers to the actual price advertisers pay for each click in pay-per-click (PPC) marketing campaigns. And there's often a strong correlation between the CPC values of a keyword and the amount of money an article based on that keyword can earn through display ad revenue and affiliate product sales.

The example you'll find next will help you understand how this all works in the *Keyword Accelerator Formula*.

To get started, I want you to compare the most important keyword metrics for these two fictitious keyword phrases:

Keyword #1: Cheap Car Insurance for Young Drivers
Search Volume: 14,000
KD Score: 15
CPC Value: $7.49

Keyword #2: Best Car Insurance for Young Drivers
Search Volume: 6,000
KD Score: 15
CPC Value: $25.89

At first glance, you may think that targeting keyword #1 would be the better option because it has a higher monthly search volume—*more than double the number of searches than keyword #2*—and an equally low KD score of 15. And that keyword strategy would definitely make sense if you were only focused on getting the maximum amount of traffic to your website without any concern for the monetary value of those visitors.

But if you're monetizing your website with display ads or affiliate products, then picking keyword #1 would actually not be the best choice.

In fact, choosing keyword #1 may cause you to miss out on a lot more display ad revenue and affiliate commissions while also requiring you to capture much more traffic than keyword #2 can provide.

Here's what I mean:

The CPC value for keyword #2 is about 245% more than keyword #1. What this reveals is that advertisers are willing to pay a lot more money to have people click on their ads that are displayed in Google's search results and the Discover Network when users are searching for the phrase "Best Car Insurance for Young Drivers" than for people who are looking for "Cheap Car Insurance for Young Drivers".

In other words, the earning potential from people who are searching online for keyword #2 is 245% higher than keyword #1.

Even though more users are looking for "Cheap Car Insurance for Young Drivers" on Google, those people are not worth as much money to advertisers that are bidding on keywords related to car insurance.

When you think about that from a financial perspective, it makes perfect sense why a car insurance company would pay a higher CPC for keyword #2. Users who are searching for the "Best Car Insurance for Young Drivers" on Google are typically not as hard-pressed on getting the lowest price possible as are the people who want to find "Cheap Car Insurance for Young Drivers". Therefore, an advertiser is willing to spend more money on each cost-per-click to acquire a customer that's searching for the "best" car insurance because the advertiser knows it can get a higher ROI from their ad spend.

Now, here's how all of this relates to the *Keyword Accelerator Formula* and why it's important to consider the CPC values of the keywords you select for your website content. By choosing keywords with higher CPC values, you can often make more money with less overall traffic by publishing content that targets those pricier keywords.

If we go back to our example, you'll understand more clearly how this works.

Although keyword #1 has 14,000 monthly searches and can drive more traffic to your website, it does so at a much lower CPC value than keyword #2 ($7.49 compared to $25.89). And through my testing and experience with monetizing websites through display ads and affiliate products, I've discovered that the CPC value has a strong correlation to the average cost-per-mile (CPM) for every 1,000 impressions each web page receives and the conversion rate for visitors purchasing products through affiliate links.

I can't stress this part about the *Keyword Accelerator Formula* enough. In my opinion, the correlation between CPC values and potential earnings is an extremely important concept to understand because it can totally transform how you approach the keyword research process to make the most money from your website.

Keyword Accelerator Strategy Guide

I'm now going to walk you through the complete process of how to put the *Keyword Accelerator Formula* into practice so you can understand exactly how to do keyword research in the fastest and most effective way.

By following these steps, each and every time you do keyword research, you can find the easiest keywords to rank that can deliver the highest traffic possible, while also helping you earn more money through display ads and affiliate commissions.

Step 1: Choose a Keyword Type to Focus On

Earlier in this playbook, you learned about the three types of keywords people search for on Google, Yahoo, and Bing, which include informational, transactional, and navigational terms.

So the first step of doing effective keyword research is to choose a single keyword type to focus on for your analysis. This will help guide your keyword research process so you don't wander off looking for random terms to target on your website or get distracted by unrelated ideas.

As a publisher who is committed to long-term success, you'll find it is much more productive to work this way and it can help you reach your income and traffic goals faster because your keyword research and content publishing strategy are not scattered.

For example, you may want to do a batch of articles that answer informational questions based on keywords that start with "what", "why", or "how". Or, you may want to do a deep dive into transactional keywords that can bring in direct sales like "best", "top", "review", "buy", or "purchase".

Whatever keyword type you choose, plan to stick with it throughout the entire first pass of the keyword research process because, as you'll see in step 7, you'll want to keep digging for more related keywords of this type to fully flesh out the topical relevance on your website to help it rank higher in the SERPs.

Here's an example of how I do this first step for SEO Chatter:

I pick a single keyword type such as informational, then choose a single question prompt to focus on like "why". Next, I move on to step 2 below to uncover all of the "why" questions that are based around a seed keyword related to the topic SEO. Only after I've completed all 7 steps for that why-based question will I then move on to another informational question prompt like "how" for the same seed keyword.

Step 2: Use a Seed Keyword to Generate Ideas

No matter which keyword research tool you use (e.g., KWFinder, LowFruits, Keysearch, or something else), they all require you to use a seed (or starting) keyword to generate the initial keyword suggestions.

Typically, the best seed keyword to use is a short or medium-tail keyword that's 2-3 words in length. This allows the keyword research tool to find the widest range of relevant phrases without being restricted by too narrow of a search.

If you were to enter in a long-tail keyword phrase (i.e., 5 words or more) as your seed keyword, then you won't get as many recommendations with the keyword research tool.

For example, a good seed keyword to find general ideas on the topic of Bluetooth headphones would simply be "Bluetooth headphones". However, typing this phrase into a keyword research tool will not help you get any closer to your end content publishing goal because it's still too vague.

As you learned in step 1 of this process, you want to narrow your search a bit more so you only get suggestions that are focused on a single keyword type (i.e., informational, transactional, or navigational).

Therefore, you should use a slightly longer seed keyword phrase with some keyword modifiers such as "best Bluetooth headphones" or "how Bluetooth headphones". These terms will allow the keyword research tool to uncover the relevant search terms for those types of keywords and filter everything else out.

Below is an example list of terms that were suggested by a keyword research tool for the seed keyword "best Bluetooth headphones". As you'll see, including a slightly longer keyword phrase that's 3 words long helped us get closer to our end goal of finding transactional-based terms to target for website content.

- best Bluetooth headphones under $100
- best Bluetooth headphones for running
- best noise cancelling Bluetooth headphones
- best waterproof Bluetooth headphones
- best in ear Bluetooth headphones

Next is an example list of terms that were suggested for the seed keyword "how Bluetooth headphones". As you'll see, only information-based keywords were returned by the keyword research tool which is exactly what we would want to get relevant terms to target for informational articles on a website.

- how do Bluetooth headphones work
- how long do Bluetooth headphones last
- how to set up Bluetooth headphones
- how to charge Bluetooth headphones
- how are Bluetooth headphones made

From those examples above, you can understand how combining a specific keyword type with a seed keyword that's relevant to your website can help generate a lot of new content ideas.

But you can't just stop the keyword research process here and start writing on these topics. Otherwise, you may find yourself putting a lot of time and effort into articles that don't generate the level of traffic or earnings you were hoping to get.

That's why it's important to follow every step of the *Keyword Accelerator Strategy* so you can find the terms that are best for your website, which steps 3-7 will help you achieve.

Step 3: Sort the List By Lowest Keyword Difficulty Score

After you've generated a good list of terms with your keyword research tool that are focused on your target keyword type, the next step is to find the terms with the lowest keyword difficulty (KD) score.

As previously mentioned in the *Keyword Accelerator Formula Overview* section, the keywords with the lowest KD scores have the least competition in search engines like Google, Yahoo, and Bing. This often means you can rank very easily for them in the search engine results pages (SERPs) without having to build a lot of backlinks.

The KD Score is primarily based on the link strength of the domains and the individual URLs ranking in the top 10 positions on the SERPs. And KD scores with the number 30 or lower often means there are one or more web pages ranking in the top positions on Google that have 0-1 total backlinks.

That metric indicates you can rank for these low KD score keywords without doing any link building at all as long as you have good on-page SEO and meet the user search intent with your written content.

It's amazing how many great—*and untapped*—keywords there are for every niche that can put your website in a deep blue ocean without very few, if any, direct competitors. And using a keyword research tool like KWFinder or Keysearch, you can instantly sort your suggested keyword list by KD score to find the easiest terms to target without wasting time or energy analyzing keywords that are too competitive in the SERPs. You simply click on the KD score column header to sort the keyword list by ascending or descending order. Then scroll down until you see the cluster of keywords with low KD scores and ignore the rest.

The KD score feature on a keyword research tool is one of the most valuable assets you can have for guiding your SEO and content publishing strategy.

But choosing keywords to target based on the KD score alone is not the best course of action for long-term traffic growth. You also need to look at the monthly search volume data for each term to truly uncover the lowest competition keywords that can drive the most traffic to your website, which you'll learn about in step 4.

Step 4: Find Keywords with the Highest Search Volume

The next step for doing effective keyword research is to look through the list of the keywords you've gathered with the lowest Keyword Difficulty (KD) Scores and find the terms that have the highest search volume.

As mentioned in the *Keyword Accelerator Formula Overview* section, these high search volume keywords offer the best chance of getting more visitors to your website with the least amount of effort.

For example, it's often better to target a keyword with a KD score of 10 and a monthly search volume of 500 than it is to go after a keyword with an equally low KD score of 10 and a search volume of 20. The amount of effort it takes to write and optimize an article is the same for both keywords because they have the same KD Score of 10. So you should always target the term that can send you the most amount of website traffic, which, in this case, would be the keyword with the 500 monthly search volume.

Next is an example of how this process looks in action when comparing two or more search terms to add to your potential keyword list. As you'll see, all of these keywords have a relatively low KD score but only the first term has substantial search volume.

With all other things being equal, it would be better to write an article focused on that keyword phrases and skip the other two because the return on investment for generating website traffic is too low to make them worth it.

Keyword: Remote controlled window blinds
KD Score: 26
Search Volume: 1,900

Keyword: Remote controlled window tint
KD Score: 18
Search Volume: 20

Keyword: Remote controlled window coverings
KD Score: 12
Search Volume: 10

At this point of the keyword research process, you'll have narrowed down your initial list of low KD score keywords to only the top terms with the highest potential search traffic. The next step you'll take is to analyze the cost-per-click value for each keyword so you can pick the terms that can deliver the highest financial reward for your content writing efforts. Otherwise, you may end up with a web page that generates a lot of monthly search traffic but doesn't earn you much money through display ads or affiliate product sales.

Step 5: Examine the Cost-Per-Click for Each Keyword

If you're monetizing a website with display ads or affiliate products, then it's crucial that you examine the cost-per-click (CPC) value for each keyword you're thinking of targeting on your website.

As mentioned in the *Keyword Accelerator Formula Overview* section, there's often a strong correlation between high CPC values and the amount of money you can earn with an article that's focused on a particular keyword with display ads and affiliate product sales.

Here's a case in point from my own SEO Chatter blog which is monetized with display ads:

I have an article targeting the keyword phrase "internal vs external links". And it brings my website several hundred visits per month from Google, Yahoo, and Bing. However, I barely earn any money at all from display ads on that page because the CPC value is less than $0.10.

While the traffic boost is a nice vanity metric to help inflate my monthly Google Analytics tracking data, the truth is the target keyword is not generating much revenue for my business. The article does help with brand awareness but it's not improving the bottom line for SEO Chatter in regards to display ad monetization.

From a pure revenue standpoint, I would have been better off ditching the term "internal vs external links" with a CPC value of $0.10 and writing a blog post that focused on a keyword with a higher CPC value like $20, $50, or more. Doing that would have given me a higher return on investment for the time it took to write a new blog post.

Instead of making a measly $1-2 per month from a post targeting "internal vs external links" with display ads, I could have targeted a higher CPC keyword that could be generating possibly $20 or more from a single page.

Because this step is so important to the future of any monetized website, I want us to look at another example of how examining the CPC values for each keyword can help you refine your content publishing strategy.

As you'll see next, the keyword phrase "how often does a dog pee" is an easy keyword to target because it has a low keyword difficulty (KD) score of 18. It also has a good search volume of 850 searches per month.

With a proper on-page SEO and writing content that meets the user search intent, you could likely win a top position for that keyword on Google, Yahoo, or Bing without building any backlinks.

But is really worth the time and trouble to get a top-ranking position?

Let's see.

Keyword: How often does a dog pee
KD Score: 18
Search Volume: 850
CPC: $0

If you consider the CPC value of the keyword phrase, then it doesn't matter how low the KD score is or how high the search volume is to make the right decision on if you should target this term or not. If you're monetizing your website through display ads or affiliate products, the answer is more often than not going to be no.

The CPC value of $0 indicates that advertisers are not willing to spend any money on acquiring customers who are searching for the phrase "how often does a dog pee" on Google, which typically correlates to an equally low cost-per-mile (CPM) for every 1,000 impressions a web page gets and the number of people who will purchase an affiliate product after landing on a web page that answers the question about the frequency of dogs peeing.

Now compare that first keyword phrase to this second one below.

The second term has an equally low KD score of 18 but a lower monthly search volume of 570. However, this keyword shows a CPC value of $3.85, which is a positive sign that advertisers are willing to pay money to get their brand in front of visitors who are searching on Google for this phrase. It also signifies that you may actually be able to earn some money from an article written on this topic through display ads and affiliate products. Therefore, it would be a much better keyword to target on your website and should be added to your final keyword list.

Keyword: How to get dog pee smell out of wood
KD Score: 18
Search Volume: 570
CPC $3.85

As a publisher, your goal should be to maximize the earnings from every visitor who lands on your website. And the CPC value can help you do that.

By only choosing keywords that can generate revenue for your business, you're not only speeding up the revenue growth of your website, but it also helps you avoid writing articles that have a high probability of being a waste of time in terms of earning money.

Now, one final word of wisdom here before we move on to step 6.

Every niche, topic, and keyword will have a varying degree of CPC values. So you'll need to pick a certain threshold as your cut off point for which keywords you're willing to target based on the CPC value.

For example, in the pet niche, you may find informational keywords that start with "what", "why", or "can" that have an average CPC value between $1-3. Therefore, you need to set your expectations appropriately. You cannot set a minimum threshold of CPC $15 at the standard value for which keywords you're going to target or not. Instead, it should be a more realistic goal like the keyword needs to have a CPC value of $2 or higher to be willing to write an article on it.

The same idea is true for higher CPC value keywords.

For example, if you're in the technology niche and you're finding a wide range of transactional keywords that start with "buy", "top", or "review", and they have an average CPC value between $20-70, then you should aim for the higher-paying keywords. The amount of time and effort it takes to write an article based on a keyword with a low KD score is the same regardless if that term has a CPC $20 or $70.

So it makes the most financial sense to set an initial threshold of CPC $60 or higher for the next batch of articles you write for your website. Then, after all of that content is published, you could work your way down to the lower CPC value keywords for additional articles.

With all that being said, just do what feels comfortable to you. There is no right or wrong answer here and you'll need to investigate the average CPC values for the keywords in your niche to find an appropriate threshold.

Once you find a good set of keywords that meet this criteria, the next step is to add them to a keyword tracking template so you can store them all in one place. This is what you'll learn how to do in step 6.

Step 6: Add the Best Terms to Your Keyword Tracking Template

After you've found a great keyword worth targeting for your website (i.e., it has a low KD score, higher search volume, and high CPC value), you'll then need to keep track of it.

Some keyword research tools have a feature that allows you to save the terms you find into a list for later recall but this option doesn't help much with building out a long-term content publishing strategy. And some tools don't even allow you to check off keywords after you've written an article about them so you don't make the mistake of accidentally targeting them again.

So the best thing you can do after finding a good set of keywords is to copy them into a keyword tracking template of your own. This method will allow you to collect all the important keyword metrics for later sorting when you get to the next stage of creating your content publishing schedule. Plus, you own that data without any risk of losing the metrics if you ever decide to stop using a particular keyword research tool.

Now, you can create your own keyword tracking template with software like Microsoft Excel or Google Sheets based on the list of keyword metrics you'll find next. Or, you can grab a copy of the pre-made tracking spreadsheet I've developed to be used alongside this playbook so you don't have to make it from scratch by purchasing the *Keyword Accelerator Cheatsheets & Tracking Templates Add-On.*

Go to this link to get your copy of the template: **seochatter.com/keywordacceleratorextras**

The spreadsheet includes a downloadable file you can open and use in Microsoft Excel or Google Sheets to track all of the optimal keywords you're uncovering during the keyword research process.

Below are the most important metrics your keyword tracking template should include, which should make up the top header columns in the spreadsheet. On the next page, you'll find a sample of of the tracking template with each column filled out with example keyword data.

- Keyword
- Type
- Search Volume
- KD Score
- CPC Value
- Scheduled

Sample Keyword Tracking Template

Keyword	Type	Search Volume	KD Score	CPC Value	Scheduled
how to grill ribs on charcoal	Informational	320	20	$2.14	Yes
how to grill frozen burgers	Informational	400	25	$1.84	Yes
best infrared grills	Transactional	550	13	$23.58	No
when is charcoal ready to cook on	Informational	110	7	$1.19	No
flattop grill for bbq	Transactional	1300	18	$31.23	No

A few notes about these columns:

- The "Keyword" column should just contain the search term.
- The "Type" column should contain variables for "Informational", "Transactional", and "Navigational" so you know what type of content the article is targeting.

Notes about the columns continued…

- The "Search Volume" column should only have the average monthly searches as reported in the keyword research tool.

- The "KD Score" column should include the keyword difficulty score if your keyword research tool shows that metric. If it doesn't, you can use your own rating system like a scale of 1-10 if you're using a tool like LowFruits that shows the number of Weak Spots in the top 10 SERP positions rather than a specific KD score.

- The "CPC Value" should contain the reported cost-per-click that advertisers are willing to spend on a particular keyword.

- The "Scheduled" column is used to keep track of the keywords you've chosen to add to your Content Publishing Schedule Template, which is explained in the next section of this playbook. This Schedule field should contain a "Yes" or "No" next to each keyword in the list to indicate which keywords have already been assigned to your Content Publishing Schedule Template so you don't write more than one article based on the same keyword.

Step 7: Dig Deeper for Related Keyword Ideas

After you've completed your initial pass through the keyword research process and copied the optimal terms into your keyword tracking template, the next thing you want to do is dig deeper to find additional related keyword ideas.

Essentially, you want to exhaust all of the relevant keywords in a particular category before going back to step 1 of the keyword research process and uncovering search terms in a new topic. The keywords you found by following steps 1 through 5 are just the starting point for building topical relevance on your website.

Topical relevance is a powerful way to outrank other websites that have higher SEO metrics than your site because you can establish yourself as having a strong authority on a specific subject.

When it comes to optimizing your website for SEO, the more content you can publish about a particular keyword topic, the easier it will be for your website to rank for related search terms in Google, Yahoo, and Bing. In other words, the website that can demonstrate more expertise on a specific topic tends to rank higher in the search engines for all web pages that are relevant to that topic.

Here's what this idea of digging deeper to find related keywords looks like in practice:

Imagine you have a website that sells remote controlled (RC) vehicles for play and sport. You then went through steps 1 to 5 of the keyword research process and found this transactional type of keyword to target: "best RC mud trucks".

Instead of just writing a single article on that topic and moving on to the next type of RC vehicle (e.g., RC planes, RC cars, or RC boats), you can use your keyword research tool to dig deeper to find other relevant terms to help build stronger topical relevance for "RC mud trucks" on your website. And you can do that by looking for both transactional and informational keywords to capture more visibility in the search engines.

You don't have to limit yourself to just the same keyword type.

For example, the list of terms you'll find next are some related keyword phrases that were found with a keyword research tool on the topic of "RC mud trucks".

- Best gas powered RC mud trucks (transactional)
- Top battery powered RC mud trucks (transactional)
- Cheap RC mud trucks (transactional)

Keywords related to RC mud trucks continued...

- RC mud truck kits (transactional)
- How to build an RC mud truck (informational)
- How to clean a muddy RC truck (informational)
- Can RC mud trucks do jumps (informational)

Now let's look at another example that applies to the topic of "email marketing".

Instead of writing a single article on general email marketing tips, you could dig deeper with your keyword research tool to find other relevant terms people are searching for on Google, Yahoo, and Bing for email marketing. Then you could write individual articles on each sub-topic to improve the topical relevance as a whole for email marketing on the website.

This SEO strategy is powerful because it not only helps you attract more website traffic by having more articles in total, but it can also improve your overall rankings in the search engines for related topics on email marketing because you've demonstrated your expertise in multiple aspects of the subject.

For example, the list of terms you'll find next are some related keyword phrases that were found with a keyword research tool on the topic of "email marketing".

Email marketing related keywords:

- Email marketing for authors
- Email marketing for agencies
- Email marketing for affiliate marketers
- Email marketing for b2b
- Email marketing for beginners
- Email marketing for lead generation
- Email marketing for non-profits
- Email marketing for real estate
- Email marketing for small business
- Email marketing for virtual events
- Email marketing for YouTube

As you can see, the opportunities for new article ideas are practically endless. There are literally hundreds of different, yet topically relevant, keywords that relate closely to the parent topic of email marketing.

That's why it's important to always dig deeper into the keywords you find that pass the test for being an optimal keyword to target (i.e., low KD score, high search volume, and high CPC value).

Doing this one extra step can help you instantly uncover a ton of other relevant keywords that you can use to take your website traffic, rankings, and earnings to the next level.

Popular Keyword Search Strings

I've included this section in the playbook to help you get started with the initial keyword research process.

One of the biggest roadblocks new publishers often have after learning the process for doing effective keyword research is figuring out what search strings should they use to find good keywords to target on their websites.

After doing keyword research for many years, I realized there are certain keyword search strings that can be used over and over again to help find popular topics to fill up an entire content publishing schedule. In fact, these are the same search strings I use for my own websites and I never run out of new article ideas.

The list you'll find next includes the most popular keyword search strings you can use to create a well-balanced website with both transactional and information content to attract visitors at various stages of the customer journey. These examples include the keyword search strings for both basic keyword research tools that only accept a seed keyword phrase and advanced keyword research tools that allow you to use a wildcard (*) to find more relevant results.

Just pick the version that works best for your chosen keyword research tool.

How to Use These Keyword Strings

Replace [keyword] with your seed keyword. For example, the seed keyword "portable air conditioner" would change the basic search string "does [keyword]" to be "does portable air conditioner". And it would change the advanced search string "how * [keyword]" to be "how * portable air conditioner".

Basic Search String	Advanced Search String
[keyword]	* [keyword] or [keyword] *
who [keyword]	who * [keyword]
what [keyword]	what * [keyword]
when [keyword]	when * [keyword]
where [keyword]	where * [keyword]
why [keyword]	why * [keyword]
how [keyword]	how * [keyword]
are [keyword]	are [keyword] *
can [keyword]	can [keyword] *
do [keyword]	do [keyword] *
does [keyword]	does [keyword] *
will [keyword]	will [keyword] *
[keyword] for	[keyword] for *

Keyword strings table continued...

Basic Search String	Advanced Search String
[keyword] vs	[keyword] vs *
[keyword] alternatives	[keyword] alternatives * or * [keyword] alternatives
[keyword] ideas	[keyword] ideas *
[keyword] ideas for	[keyword] ideas for *
best [keyword]	best [keyword] *
best [keyword] for	best [keyword] for *
top [keyword]	top [keyword] *
top [keyword] for	top [keyword] for *
cheap [keyword]	cheap [keyword] *
cheap [keyword] for	cheap [keyword] for *
[keyword] review	[keyword] review *

Bonus Tip: Steal Your Competitors' Keywords

An additional feature that keyword research tools like KWFinder and Keysearch include is the ability to analyze any domain or URL for its top-ranking keywords.

This includes your competitors' websites.

Doing competitive analysis like this is another way to find relevant keywords to target without having to think up new ideas. It also helps you discover easy-to-rank keywords that are bringing organic search traffic to your competitors that you can also try to capture for your own website.

Some people refer to this keyword research strategy as a "competitor gap analysis" while others simply call it "stealing your competitor's keywords".

But no matter what it's called, the ultimate goal is the same:

To discover great keyword ideas with very little effort.

A competitive analysis like this helps you identify gaps in keywords that your competitors are ranking for—*and you are not*—that you can create content for to hopefully rank higher in the search engines than them as a way to steal their organic search traffic and ranking positions.

To use this method, all you have to do is enter a competitor's domain or specific URL into the appropriate search field of a keyword research tool that supports it and then click the "Find Keywords" button. The tool will then scan the website and fetch all of the relevant keywords from its database that are being tracked across the entire domain or a specific URL.

After that keyword list is returned, you then go through the same process for evaluating any keyword based on the *Keyword Accelerator Formula* you learned in this playbook.

You want to select keyword phrases that meet this basic formula and skip the rest:

Low KD + High SV + High CPC = Optimal KW

SECTION 2
CONTENT PLANNING

What Is a Content Publishing Plan?

A content publishing plan is a written schedule of when, and in which order, you plan to publish upcoming content on your website.

Also known as an editorial calendar, a content publishing plan for websites typically includes the due date for upcoming articles, published status, target keyword, keyword type, and URL for the published content.

The basic process for creating a content publishing schedule consists of a few steps:

- Pick a time frame for an upcoming set of articles.
- Choose how many articles will be published.
- Arrange the articles by the due date based on the keyword type or topic.

Why Is a Content Publishing Schedule Important?

A content publishing schedule is important because it allows you to organize your article ideas in a way that gives your website purpose and direction. It also helps you to optimize your content over the long-term for specific keyword topics as planned sets (or themes) so you're not posting randomly without any particular goal in mind.

Planning out your content schedule in advance is also the most effective way to stay on track as a website publisher without taking unnecessarily long breaks between publishing articles.

One of the hardest parts of being a blogger, niche website builder, or affiliate marketer is posting content on a consistent basis. And without a proper plan in place, you typically won't be able to maximize your website's growth potential because you don't have a schedule in place to meet certain content deadlines.

Setting up a content publishing schedule and sticking to it is one of the top secrets of successful online publishers. And it's a simple strategy like this that helps keep serious website owners accountable and on track to achieve long-term growth from their efforts.

Creating a Content Publishing Schedule

This section will teach you how to create a content publishing schedule based on the list of keywords you've found and added to your keyword tracking template.

What often happens with new website owners and bloggers is that they come up with a good list of optimal keywords to target but they don't know which terms to write articles about first or how many new posts they should publish per week. These stumbling blocks often lead to an erratic content publishing schedule and a haphazard approach to the articles they post on their website.

Next, you'll learn the step-by-step process for how to take the list of keywords you have in your keyword tracking template and put them into a content plan that works best for your schedule and makes the most sense for your website.

Step 1: Choose a Publishing Time Frame

The first step of creating a content publishing schedule is to choose a time frame to publish a new batch of articles.

You could select 1 week, 2 weeks, 1 month, 3 months, 6 months, or even an entire year.

No matter what time frame you choose, just make sure to stick to it. Consistency and meeting your content publishing deadlines are essential for having long-term success.

For example, I like to set up a publishing schedule for my websites that spans a 3-month time frame. This strategy allows me to set up a 90-day plan so I know exactly what I'm going to write about without guessing each week. Plus, it lets me batch my keyword topics together so I can focus on one particular topic during each quarter of the year. (You'll learn more about this strategy in step 4.)

Step 2: Decide on the Number of Articles to Be Published

The next step in planning out your content schedule is to decide on the number of articles to be published on your website within the chosen time frame.

Your target goal could be anything you're comfortable with, such as 4 articles over 30 days, 12 articles within 2 months, 60 articles in 3 months, 500 articles in one year, etc.

Whatever your goal is, you need to make sure you have enough keywords in your keyword tracking template to cover the chosen time frame.

For example, you couldn't set out to publish 30 articles in the next 2 months if you only have 10 keywords in your keyword tracking template. To meet that goal, you would have to go back through the keyword research process to find 20 more keywords to reach your target of 30 articles (10 + 20 = 30).

To give you a real-life example of how this step works for the SEO Chatter website, I try to publish 5 articles per week on the blog. This averages out to be 20 articles per month. Therefore, the goal I set for the number of articles I want to publish in a 3-month time frame is 60 articles (20 x 3 = 60).

Once you have your ideal number of articles to published figured out, you can then move on to step 3 to start planning out the actual content publishing schedule for your website.

Step 3: Plan Out Your Content Publishing Schedule

Now that you have your publishing time frame established and the total number of articles you want to publish, the next step is to plan out the specific dates for your content to go live on your website.

The easiest way to get started here is to take the number of articles you want to publish and divide it by your chosen time frame.

For example, publishing 8 articles over a 4-week time frame would turn out to be 2 articles per week ($8 \div 4 = 2$).

Next, you need to pick certain days of the week you want to publish the content on your website (i.e., Sunday through Saturday). That way, you can stay consistent with your publishing schedule to ensure you meet your weekly content goals.

If we take the previous example of publishing 2 articles per week, a good schedule could be Mondays and Fridays to get that content published on the website. And each week, you would make sure to have those articles finished and ready to go live on those two days.

However, just do what works best for you. If it's publishing several articles in a single day each week, then that's fine too. So is publishing articles on back-to-back days or even random days during each week of the month. There is no right or wrong answer here.

The ultimate goal of this step is to help you publish a specific quantity of content on a weekly basis so you can meet your overall content publishing goal. And all you need to achieve that is to take the total number of articles you want to publish in your chosen time frame, then divide that amount by the number of weeks in your schedule.

After you do that, you can assign specific due dates for each new piece of content to be published on your website.

A content planning template is an essential item to use to keep you on track. (More on that in just a bit.) And at this planning stage of the process, all you have to do is go through the template and assign the due dates for upcoming articles you want to publish.

That's it.

Nothing else is required right now because you're just trying to map out your future plan for when content should go live on your website.

Let's say you chose to publish 1 article per week on Mondays for the month of January. Below would an example list of those dates based on the current year's calendar:

- 1/3/22
- 1/10/22
- 1/17/22
- 1/24/22
- 1/31/22

Now, you can create your own content scheduling template with software like Microsoft Excel or Google Sheets based on the items you see in the example spreadsheet you'll find next.

Or, you can grab a copy of the pre-made scheduling spreadsheet I've developed to be used alongside this playbook so you don't have to make it from scratch by purchasing the *Keyword Accelerator Cheatsheets & Tracking Templates Add-On.*

Go to this link to get your copy of the template: **seochatter.com/keywordacceleratorextras**

The spreadsheet includes a downloadable file you can open and use in Microsoft Excel or Google Sheets to set up your entire publishing plan for each month of the year.

Here's a sample of how your content publishing schedule should look at this stage of the process:

Due Date	Status	Keyword	Type	URL
1/3/22				
1/10/22				
1/17/22				
1/24/22				
1/31/22				

In step 5, you'll get an explanation for each of the column headers as well as a sample template completely filled out for you to use as a quick reference guide.

But for now, you just need to go through the content publishing schedule template and assign the due dates for when you want the articles to go live on your website over your chosen time frame.

Step 4: Pick the Right Publishing Strategy for Your Website

Before we start putting keywords and other data into the content scheduling template, you need to choose how you're going to batch your content together inside the plan.

There are two strategies you can use to set up your content publishing schedule that can help you take advantage of the SEO benefits of topical relevance.

As mentioned in step 7 of the *Keyword Accelerator Strategy Guide*, when it comes to optimizing your website for SEO, the more content you can publish about a particular keyword topic or type, the easier it will be for your website to rank for those related terms in Google, Yahoo, and Bing.

To help you achieve those kinds of results, the following two keyword batching strategies can help you plan out your content schedule based on topical relevance.

You can choose either strategy you like best, but you may want to look over the list of keywords in your keyword tracking template before making a final decision. That's because you need to make sure you have enough of the same types or topics of keywords to make each method work.

Option 1: Batch Keyword Types Together

With this first strategy, you're putting keywords together in your content publishing schedule based on the keyword type (e.g., transactional or informational). This method is good for publishers who like to stick to a certain theme for their website articles until they move on to the next content vertical.

For example, you may decide to only publish content over your chosen time frame that's transactional-based.

Below is a sample batch of keywords that fits this criteria for a website that reviews a broad range of home products. Notice how each keyword phrase has a transactional search intent, such as "best", "top", "cheap", "reviews", and "for sale".

- best robot vacuums
- top blinds for children's bedroom
- cheap stainless steel dishwashers
- automatic espresso machine reviews
- dining room chairs for sale

Now here's a sample batch of keywords that only targets informational content. Notice how it sticks to one specific topic (i.e., robot vacuums) and focuses solely on informational-based keywords, such as "types", "who", "how", "can", and "why". This fully maximizes the SEO power of topical relevance to help the website become a trusted authority on robot vacuums.

- types of robot vacuums
- who makes robot vacuums
- how to choose a robot vacuum
- can robot vacuums clean in corners
- why are robot vacuums round

Option 2: Batch Keyword Topics Together

With this second strategy, you're not worried at all about keyword types when planning out your content schedule. Instead, you're picking a specific topic to publish a batch of articles on that completely fleshes out a single category of content.

This method is good for publishers who like to exhaust every option for a narrow topic until they move on to the next content vertical.

For example, let's say you only wanted to publish content over a chosen time frame that's focused on the topic of "blinds for children's bedrooms". As you've already learned, this strategy can help improve the topical relevance of your website so it can rank easier, and higher, for related search terms.

Next is a sample batch of keywords that fits this criteria while targeting both transactional and informational keywords on the topic of "blinds for children's bedrooms":

- top blinds for children's bedroom
- cheap blinds for children's bedroom
- best vinyl blinds for children's bedroom
- best cordless blinds for children's bedroom
- best wood blinds for children's bedroom

Keyword batch continued…

- what kind of blinds are good for children's bedrooms
- how to measure blinds for children's bedroom
- are blinds safe for children's bedrooms
- children's bedroom blind ideas
- children's bedroom blind alternatives

The sky's the limit for how many articles you want to batch together like this before moving on to a new content vertical. However, the more you can do the better it will be for your website's overall rankings.

A good number to aim for is at least 5-10 articles per topic at a bare minimum to help establish topical relevance for SEO.

That's why it's important to follow step 7 of the first section of this playbook, Keyword Accelerator Strategy Guide, to dig deep to find as many related keywords as possible before moving on to another keyword type or topic. By fully exhausting your search for every optimal keyword available, you can set yourself up to completely dominate a particular category of content in a niche.

Step 5: Arrange Your Keywords In the Content Publishing Schedule

By this point in the process, you've completed 90% of the content planning work. So let's do a quick recap of what you've already accomplished:

- Chosen a publishing time frame.
- Decided on the number of articles you're going to publish.
- Planned out which days of the week you're going to publish content and the specific due dates for articles to go live on the site.
- Selected how you're going to batch your content together based on keyword types and topics.

The only missing piece here is arranging the chosen keywords from your keyword tracking template in the correct order so they're mapped out to the specific dates on your content publishing schedule.

Once you do that, you'll know exactly what you're going to write about, in which order, and when each article is due to be published on the website.

This will give you a finalized plan of action to follow to keep yourself accountable for meeting your content publishing goals.

As explained back in step 3, you can create your own content publishing schedule template with software like Microsoft Excel or Google Sheets based on the items you see listed next. Or, you can grab a copy of the pre-made scheduling spreadsheet I've developed to be used alongside this playbook so you don't have to make it from scratch by purchasing the *Keyword Accelerator Cheatsheets & Tracking Templates Add-On.*

Go to this link to get your copy of the template: **seochatter.com/keywordacceleratorextras**

The spreadsheet includes a downloadable file you can open and use in Microsoft Excel or Google Sheets to set up your entire publishing plan for each month of the year.

Your content scheduling template should contain five columns with the following list of headers to record the most important data for your chosen keywords:

- Due Date
- Status
- Keyword
- Type
- URL

Here's a sample of how the content publishing schedule should be set up with each of the rows filled out where it's appropriate:

Due Date	Status	Keyword	Type	URL
1/3/22	Published	types of skateboards	Informational	https://domain.com/types-of-skateboards
1/10/22	Not Published	best skateboards for beginners	Transactional	
1/17/22	Not Published	history of skateboarding	Informational	
1/24/22	Not Published	how to get into skateboarding	Informational	
1/31/22	Not Published	best skateboard gear for beginners	Transactional	

A few notes about these columns:

- The "Due Date" column includes the target date you want the content focused on each keyword to be published each week.

- The "Status" column should contain one of two options: "Published" or "Not Published" to indicate the status of the article.

- The "Keyword" column is where you put the target keyword phrase.

Notes about the columns continued...

- The "Type" column should contain variables for "Information", "Transactional", and "Navigational" so you know what type of content the article is targeting. This can help you during the process of batching your keywords if you're concerned about sorting your content by types.

- The "URL" column is where you'll put a direct link to the article after it has been published for easy reference.

Important Reminder: As you're selecting keywords from your keyword tracking template to put into your content publishing schedule, you need to update the "Scheduled" column in the keyword tracking template for each term you use with a "Yes" or "No" to indicate which keywords have already been assigned to your content publishing schedule. This will keep you from accidentally writing more than one article based on the same keyword.

NEXT STEPS
FOR SUCCESS

Congratulations!

You now know what it takes to do effective keyword research and strategic content planning for your website. By putting everything you learned in this *Keyword Accelerator Playbook* into practice, you can experience better keyword rankings, more traffic, and higher earnings with a content publishing schedule that works best for you and your business.

But where do you go from here?

I'd like to suggest a few options that can further help to maximize your website's growth.

Improve Your On-Page SEO

The next step is to write your SEO-optimized articles and get them published on your website.

However, without proper on-page SEO your articles will have a tougher time ranking on the first page of Google, Yahoo, and Bing for your target keywords. And that can seriously set you back from all the time and effort you put into finding great SEO keywords for your website.

If you need help learning how to improve your on-page SEO, then I invite you to check out my ***Mastering On-Page SEO course***.

Inside, you'll discover my proven system that takes all the guesswork out of how to rank more content on the first page of Google using on-page SEO strategies alone.

It's literally the exact same methods I use as a professional SEO expert to optimize every article I publish day in and day out.

To get a special discount on the ***Mastering On-Page SEO course*** go to seochatter.com/masteringseo and use coupon code **ONPAGEACCELERATOR** during checkout.

Improve Your Affiliate Content

Are you running an affiliate website or have any affiliate content on your blog?

And are you monetizing it with Amazon Associates, ShareAsale, Impact Radius, Commission Junction, or any other affiliate partnership?

If so, then you know firsthand how valuable it can be to publish top 10 style affiliate product review guides. However, a lot of affiliate marketers are creating this type of content in a way that doesn't rank well on Google and has poor conversion rates.

That's why I created a set of **Affiliate Buying Guide Templates** to help take all of the guesswork out of how to structure and optimize an affiliate buying guide to help it rank higher on Google and make more money with this monetization method.

Inside this template pack, you'll find my proven outlines for how to set up a top 10 style affiliate product review page that can get you more targeted keyword traffic and higher conversions with less work.

To get a special discount on the **Affiliate Buying Guide Templates** go to seochatter.com/affiliatetemplates and use coupon code **AFFILIATEACCELERATOR** during checkout.

Book a 1-on-1 Consultation

My top goal with the *Keyword Accelerator Playbook* is to teach you everything you need to know do to better SEO keyword research and create a content publishing plan that works best for your website.

However, you may want some extra help with understanding the playbook material or putting it into action on your website to fully take it to the next level.

If that's the case, then I can help you get unstuck with a 1-on-1 consultation call.

On the call, we can also talk about other ways to reach your website and income goals faster—*and with less effort*—using SEO, content writing, and other proven strategies for growth.

To book a 1-hour consultation call, just send me an email at **stephen@seochatter.com** to discuss the next steps.

I can't wait to help unlock your website's full potential!

Your SEO Mentor,
Stephen Hockman
Founder of SEO Chatter

MORE ABOUT THE CHEATSHEETS & TRACKING TEMPLATES

As an additional resource for the *Keyword Accelerator Playbook*, I've developed a set of cheatsheets and tracking templates you can use to get more value out of this guide.

This set of downloadable files can be helpful if you don't want to create your own printable step-by-step guides or tracking spreadsheets from scratch that are referenced in the playbook.

You'll find a summary of each cheatsheet and tracking template includes on the next page. And if you'd like to purchase this add-on, then go to this link: **seochatter.com/keywordacceleratorextras**

Keyword Research Cheatsheet

You can download and print out this cheatsheet to have alongside you while you're doing the keyword research process. With this cheatsheet by your side, you won't miss any of the steps necessary for putting the *Keyword Accelerator Formula* into practice.

Keyword Tracking Template

You can download this template to keep track of the best keywords you find with a keyword research tool as well as their important metrics. It can be opened with any spreadsheet software like Microsoft Excel or Google Sheets.

Content Publishing Schedule Cheatsheet

You can download and print out this cheatsheet to have alongside you while you're setting up your content publishing schedule. With this cheatsheet by your side, you won't miss any of the steps necessary for planning out your content schedule so it works best for you and your website.

Content Publishing Schedule Template

You can download this template to plan out your content schedule based on the keywords you've gathered in the keyword tracking template. It can be opened with any spreadsheet software like Microsoft Excel or Google Sheets.

ABOUT THE AUTHOR

Stephen Hockman has been doing SEO since 2005 and is the founder of SEO Chatter. As an SEO writer and course instructor, his passion is to help others master search engine optimization so they can get higher rankings and more targeted traffic for their websites.

You can find Stephen sharing daily SEO news and tips at **seochatter.com**.

If you'd like to join his exclusive newsletter so you don't miss out on any of his latest SEO advice, then go to **seochatter.com/subscribe** to get on the list.

Printed in Great Britain
by Amazon

81628513R00071